D0276114

THE
RUSSIAN
WAR

THE RUSSIAN WAR: 1941-1945
EDITED BY DANIELA MRÁZKOVÁ AND VLADIMÍR REMEŠ
TEXT BY A.J.P. TAYLOR

Jonathan Cape
Thirty Bedford Square London

First published in Great Britain 1978
Copyright © 1975 by Daniela Mrázková and Vladimír Remeš
Preface, text and notes copyright © 1977, 1978 by A. J. P. Taylor
Designed by David King
First published in Czechoslovakia under the title *Fotografovali Válku*
Jonathan Cape Ltd, 30 Bedford Square, London WC1

British Library Cataloguing in Publication Data
The Russian war, 1941–1945
1. World War, 1939–1945 – Campaigns – Pictorial works
2. Russia – Armed Forces – Pictorial works
I. Mrázková, Daniela II. Remeš, Vladimír
III. Taylor, Alan John Percivale
940.54′12′47   D764
ISBN 0-224-01587-7
Printed in England by Jolly & Barber Limited, Rugby

CONTENTS

PREFACE

There are many thousand Soviet photographs of the second world war. They have been exhibited all over the world and have served as illustrations of innumerable books. The present volume, first published in Czechoslovakia in 1975, has a different purpose. It is not a history. It is designed to show the artistic merits and the human purpose of Soviet cameramen. There were some

two hundred Soviet photographers serving with the armies, among them five women, one of whom features in this book. Some of them were tied to a particular front; some ranged more widely. The photographs are grouped to illustrate the successive phases of the war and are presented more or less in chronological order.

The events of the Great Patriotic War are

still vivid in Soviet Russia and the Communist countries of eastern Europe. Here they are less familiar. I have therefore provided a brief narrative as introduction to each episode from Moscow to Berlin and have added to this some account of the cameramen particularly involved. Brief biographical notes on all the photographers appear at the end of the book.

◀ Anatoli Garanin: Kerch, spring 1942

A PEOPLE AT WAR

In the second world war the camera came of age as an instrument of information and propaganda. Cameramen recorded the German offensive in France and the pathetic columns of refugees. They recorded the Japanese attack on Pearl Harbor and the sinking of the *Prince of Wales*. They recorded the battle of El Alamein and the landings on D-day. They also showed life on the home front: the effects of bombing, the queues, the workers in the factories. There have been innumerable illustrated books on the war and its various aspects. I myself wrote one of them and of course looked at many more photographs than I used. I have helped the writers of other illustrated histories. I imagined that I had got beyond surprise and knew all the visual aspects of the second world war.

I was wrong. The collection of Soviet photographs which this book presents has stunned and inspired me. It has no parallel. This is not a record of war from on high as seen by the commanders of the time and by historians later. It is the record of a people at war and of their experiences. We often say that there was no difference in the second world war

between the fighting fronts and the home front. But of course there was. The British people suffered much from the war. Half a million houses were destroyed and 60,000 people killed by bombing attacks. Conditions were often hard. But in many ways British people lived well. There was more social equality than at any time in British history and the British people were never so well nourished as in 1943.

Russian losses were far more savage. One out of every 22 Russian soldiers was killed, as against one out of every 150 soldiers with the British. In all 6 million Russian soldiers were killed in battle and 14 million soldiers and civilians were murdered by the Germans. If British casualties had been the same, we should have lost 5 million dead instead of 300,000. In Soviet Russia 1,710 towns, 70,000 villages, 6 million houses and 31,850 factories were destroyed. The fighting front was not somewhere remote, read about in the newspapers. It swept across most of European Russia, reaching towns and cities hundreds of miles from the frontiers. No civilian lived securely behind the lines. The battles were fought in the midst of civilian communities and if a battle was lost the civilians who had not fled passed under the rule of savage German conquerors who treated them like dumb cattle to be exploited and slaughtered.

This was the war that Soviet cameramen

set out to record. British and American cameramen were devoted reporters. They came out to the front. Many of them were killed. But their purpose was to record what was happening for the benefit of people at home. For the Soviet cameramen the war was everywhere. Their purpose was not to serve a distant public, but to assert the deep involvement of the Soviet people in the war. There was of course a propaganda purpose: to stress the unity of the Soviet people under suffering. Soviet cameramen had always seen themselves as artists. Though most of them worked for weekly illustrated magazines, they did not regard themselves as journalists using a different medium. They were creative artists, along with the great Soviet film directors. Indeed their works have the quality of great Soviet films such as *Battleship Potemkin* or *Storm over Asia*. I would go even further. These Soviet photographs are a twentieth-century equivalent of *War and Peace*, transmuting human experiences into a vision of grandeur.

This is a book devoted to the Soviet people. There are no great figures: no Stalin, no generals, no glittering uniforms. This is a war of the anonymous masses. There are only two individuals named throughout the entire array of photographs: a battalion commander (p. 87) and a humble partisan (p. 31) who was killed shortly after the photograph was 9

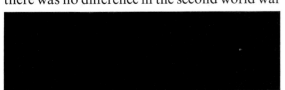

◀ **Mikhail Trakhman: Evacuation**

taken. There is one exception. One high officer is named and photographed. But this is not a Russian general. It is Field Marshal Paulus emerging from his dug-out to surrender after the battle of Stalingrad, an exception that indeed proves the rule.

Though the photographs are arranged more or less in chronological order, the book does not seek to present a coherent history of the Great Patriotic War as the Russians call it. Often no doubt no photographer was present, as in the first battles on the frontier when the Soviet armies were taken by surprise. Often mere war pictures as we should call them have been deliberately left out. There is nothing for instance about the battle of Kursk in July 1943, the greatest tank battle of all time and the turning point of the war. Such photographs would have gone against the spirit of the book which is devoted to the Soviet people and not to the strategical designs of generals. For obvious reasons there are no pictures of the German conquerors. There are pictures of the Germans in defeat and these are informed with deep human sympathy (p. 137). At the end of the book (pp. 138–43), the Soviet press photographers make a belated appearance, asserting perhaps after all that they made the pictures.

These photographs do not only depict the most destructive war of all time. They also depict a great people who have had a harsh history. These are a people inured to suffering. The note is often one of sorrow and mourning. The vast spaces of Russia add a further note of human beings astray, spaces so vast that human beings seem almost out of place. But there is a constant reassertion of human sentiments. There is grief but there is also affection and a sense of community. Few pictures are so simple and so touching as the two entitled 'Thank you, son' (pp. 91, 95). Thank you for what — for winning a battle or thank you for being alive and for briefly coming home? It does not matter. This is the universal theme that runs through the ages, the love of a mother for her son.

For most of the time in this book the Soviet people appear solemn, and they had every reason to be. But the soldiers, though stern, are never downcast. They are determined to defeat the invader and to drive him out. I remember at the height of the war meeting a Swiss diplomat who had recently returned from Berlin. He told me that a German officer said to him: 'We thought that we were the hardest soldiers in the world, but the Russians are harder than we are.' And so it proved, to the salvation of Soviet Russia and of all the world. Despite appearances the Soviet people are not always solemn. They too can be gay in victory, as the Stalingrad-to-Berlin dance (p. 125) demonstrates. In one way their gaiety is strikingly different from that of most soldiers in other countries. When they rejoice they play Beethoven (p. 60) or Tchaikovsky (p. 127).

The Soviet people did not endure the second world war for the sake of conquest or in order to spread Communism. They fought for their homes and for a secure, peaceful existence. If they had any aim beyond their own frontiers it was to liberate other people from Nazi tyranny, the worst and most brutal system of modern times. Thirty years afterwards we often forget how much the Soviet people did for Europe and for all of us. The Soviet armies for most of the war contended against nine-tenths of the German army and never against less than three-quarters of it. They carried the heat of the day. Without the Soviet contribution victory in the second world war would have taken much longer if it could have been achieved at all. Yet as soon as the war ended all this was swept aside. Soviet policy was regarded with suspicion, and there began the Cold War — in my opinion the greatest disaster of our lifetime. The Soviet Union is a World Power, asserting its equality with the only other World Power, the United States. But how could a people who suffered twenty million dead or Soviet statesmen who saw their state come near to destruction seek another great war? They seek security for themselves and others. The Soviet political system has great faults. It is often oppressive and sometimes brutal. But the greatest crime of the Soviet Union in western eyes is to have no capitalists and no landlords. Such at any rate is my view, consistently held for the last thirty years. If this book does something to dispel western suspicions of the Soviet Union it will have achieved its purpose and I shall have achieved my humbler purpose in writing this introduction. Those who look at these photographs assembled here will, I hope, be moved. They will be inspired by the display of humanity under stress. Above all they will perhaps agree that the Soviet people are a great people who deserve our sympathy and friendship.

◀ **Mikhail Savin: Tanks in action, 1943**

INVASION, 1941

The German invasion of Russia began without warning on 22 June 1941. The inhabitants of Moscow were taken by surprise (pp. 14, 15), as was Stalin himself. Much of the Soviet air force was destroyed on the ground. The Germans took over half a million prisoners. By the end of July the German Army Group Centre was at Smolensk. Their northern army was approaching Leningrad and their southern army was approaching Kiev. The Germans had expected the Soviet armies to disintegrate under such defeats as the French armies had done in the previous year. Instead the Soviet front was still unbroken and new armies were coming into action.

The Germans halted for a month while considering what to do next, a loss of precious time. On 23 August Hitler decided against a direct advance on Moscow and ordered instead an invasion of the Ukraine. Again there were great German victories: nearly a million prisoners taken; the Ukraine, the Donets basin and most of the Crimea occupied. Soviet Russia would have lost all its industrial strength if much of it had not already been moved beyond the Urals. At the end of September the German advance on Moscow was resumed. Once more there were great German victories: eight Soviet armies were destroyed. Hitler announced: 'The enemy is broken and will never be in a position to rise again.'

In Moscow there was panic. Crowds besieged the railway stations and the trains bound for the east. Martial law was proclaimed and the political police opened fire. The Soviet government moved to Kuibyshev. But Stalin remained in Moscow. On 6 November he addressed the Moscow Soviet, meeting in an underground railway station. On 7 November he took the salute at the traditional military parade, somewhat diminished in scale, in the Red Square (p. 35). On 2 December the Germans came within sight of Moscow. They could go no farther. The German attack was broken off. On 5 December Zhukov ordered a general offensive on the Moscow Front (pp. 36–9). The Germans were driven back. Though they then held their positions until the thaw came, their hopes of a quick victory faded. The Blitzkrieg was over.

From the first days of the war partisan groups were organized behind the German lines. Mikhail Trakhman was assigned to work with these groups. The partisans gave him a personal bodyguard and had both his camera and boxes containing exposed film wrapped with grenades so that all confidential material could be easily destroyed. When they were facing a dangerous situation, one of these guards said to him, 'Don't worry, Misha, we won't let them take you alive.' Trakhman's most striking picture is of a partisan, Alexei Grinchuk (p. 31), taken on the Leningrad front at six in the morning in June 1942. Grinchuk suddenly said to Trakhman who was lying beside him, 'Take a picture of me.' Trakhman did so. Soon after this fighting broke out. Grinchuk was wounded and had to be left behind. As the Nazis closed in on him he shouted 'Prostitye' ('Excuse me') and pulled the pin of his hand grenade. This is a heroic story though I wonder who there was standing by to witness it.

Trakhman states: 'I don't feel that I have yet managed to come to grips with the war nor have I depicted it in all its horror. This does not represent my admiration for war but for peace. It is my desire to create a textbook for young people so that they will not forget.'

Max Alpert: Late autumn ▶

14   **Ivan Shagin: Moscow, 22 June 1941**

Yevgeni Khaldei:
Moscow, 22 June 1941, ten minutes after noon

Ivan Shagin:
In the village of Yushkovo, Moscow region, 1941   15

Galina Sankova: A simple memorial

Mikhail Trakhman: Autumn 1941▶

Anatoli Garanin: Air raid, Ukraine

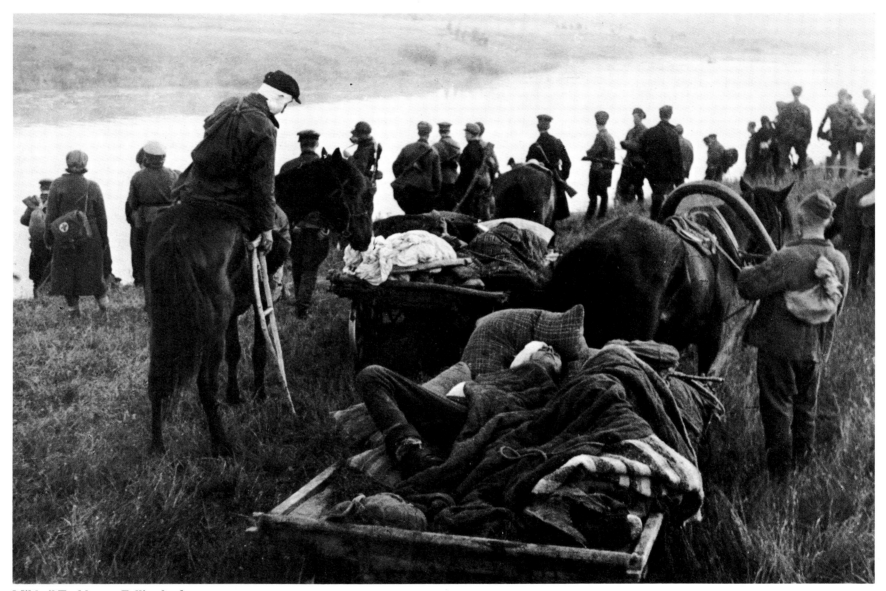

Mikhail Trakhman: Falling back

Anatoli Garanin: Crime and punishment, Briansk front

Anatoli Garanin: Near the north-western front

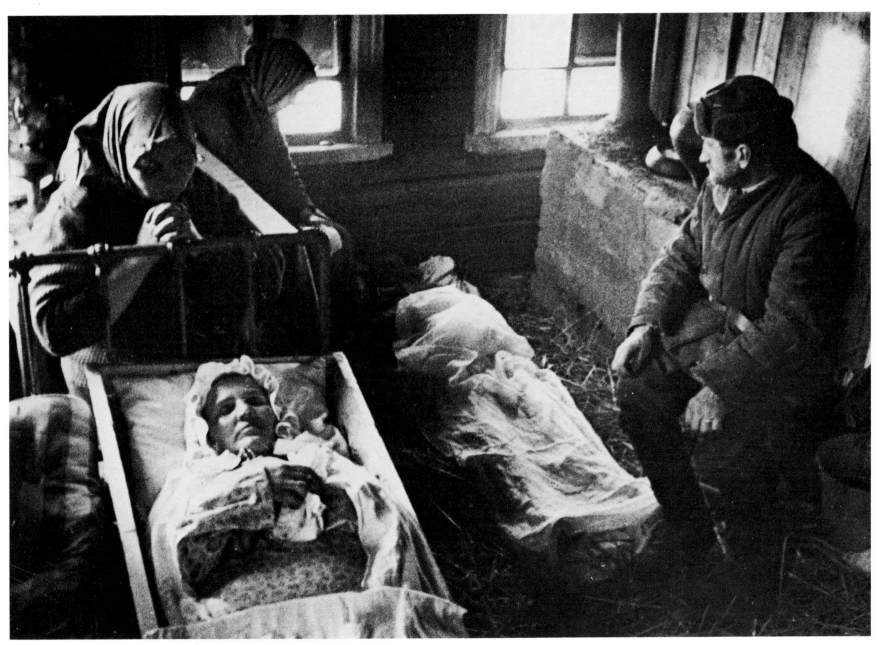

Galina Sankova: Yushkovo village farmers

24 **Mikhail Trakhman: Evacuation**

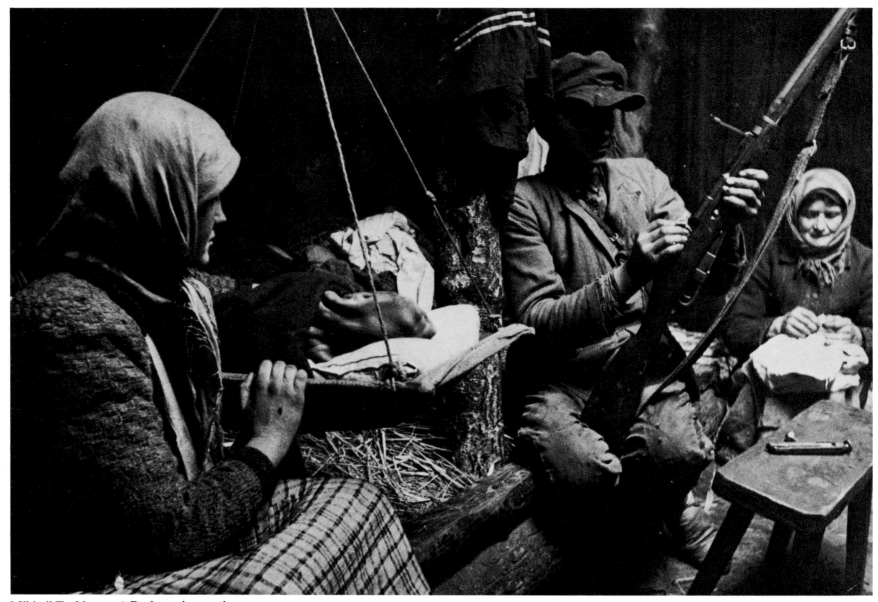

Mikhail Trakhman: A Byelorussian partisan

Mikhail Trakhman: Field hospital

Mikhail Trakhman: Bread for the partisans

Mikhail Trakhman: The partisans attack ▶

Mikhail Trakhman: End for the Germans

32 **Alexander Ustinov: Moscow 1941**

Dmitri Baltermants: The trail of war

Alexander Ustinov: Muscovites digging trenches to stop the tanks

Alexander Ustinov: Tanks in Moscow, 7 November 1941 ▶

Dmitri Baltermants: Moscow, 7 November 1941

35

Anatoli Garanin: A breach in the blockade, Volkhov front

Ivan Shagin: 40°-below-zero weather, Moscow, December 1941▶

Galina Sankova: Ill-equipped for Russian soil, December 1941
◀**Alexander Ustinov: Fighting outside Moscow**

39

LENINGRAD

Leningrad fought a war all its own. German armies reached the suburbs of Leningrad at the beginning of September 1941. German tanks attempted to force their way into the city streets. After a month's fighting they were stopped and never tried to break in again. But Leningrad was almost completely surrounded and was kept going only by supplies brought on railway tracks laid across Lake Ladoga when it froze (p. 43). The siege of Leningrad continued until January 1944. Out of the three million inhabitants over a million died of starvation and hardship. Yet life went on. Schools remained open except in the coldest weather. Factories still kept working hours. Leningrad sustained its name as the Hero City.

Boris Kudoyarov was sent to Leningrad on the first day of the war and remained there throughout the 900 days of its siege. He was therefore in the unique position of serving on a single front and of experiencing all the bitter life which he photographed. During his time in Leningrad he took 3,000 pictures, devoted to the city's heroic resistance.

Boris Kudoyarov: Pulkovo region, December 1941 ▶

◀ **Boris Kudoyarov: Leningrad 1941**

Boris Kudoyarov: The road across Lake Ladoga, 1941

Anatoli Garanin: Leningrad front, winter 1941–2
◀ **Mikhail Savin: Outside Vitebsk**

Boris Kudoyarov: Nievsky Prospect
◀ **Boris Kudoyarov: The barricade at Gatchina**

Boris Kudoyarov: Air raid, Leningrad

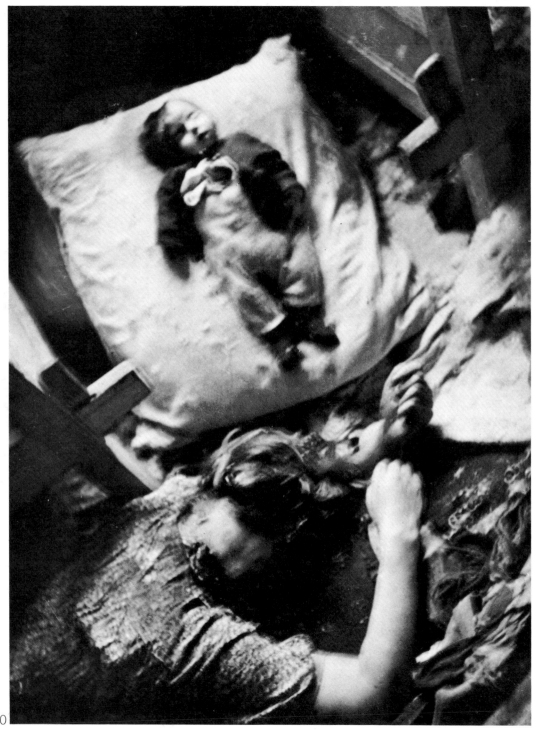

Boris Kudoyarov:
1,300,000 died during the 900-day siege of Leningrad
Boris Kudoyarov: Volkovo Cemetery, 1942 ▶

52 Mikhail Trakhman: Nievsky Prospect, 1942　　　　　　　　　　**Boris Kudoyarov: Nievsky Prospect, 1941 ▶**

FAILED OFFENSIVE: KERCH, SPRING 1942

Stalin was misled by the check to the Germans in front of Moscow. He believed that the time had already come for a general offensive to drive them off Russian soil. In the spring of 1942 three offensives were ordered. They were conducted in the old bull-headed way with Stalin insisting that they must be pressed at all costs. All three were total failures. Outside Leningrad the Russians lost an entire army, and Vlasov, its commander, deliberately surrendered to the Germans with the intention of leading an anti-Stalinist army of liberation. In the Crimea, where Sebastopol was under siege, a landing was made on the peninsula of Kerch in order to relieve the city. In May the Germans struck back. Kerch had to be evacuated with

the loss of 176,000 men and 350 tanks.

The worst disaster was the attempt to retake Kharkov in the Ukraine. Here the Russians pushed 600 tanks into a salient just when German forces were moving to eliminate it. The generals on the spot proposed to withdraw. Stalin forbade them to do so. The entire Russian front collapsed. Over 1,000 tanks were lost and 240,000 prisoners were taken. This was a disaster as great as those of 1941. It was also the last.

Most of the photographs in this section come from the Kerch peninsula, and are the work of Dmitri Baltermants. He has written: 'War, is, above all, grief. I photographed non-stop for years and I know that in all that time I

produced only five or six real photographs. War is not for photography. If, heaven forbid, I had to photograph war again, I would do it quite differently. I agonize now at the thought of all the things that I did not photograph.'

The series Baltermants took at Kerch, which he called 'Searching for loved ones' and 'Grief' (pp. 61–5), were a climax of his art. No photographs have penetrated more deeply into the nature of war. These pictures later established his fame as one of the greatest war photographers.

In a further series (pp. 67–71), Alexander Uzlyan, who was attached to the Black Sea Fleet throughout the war, displays the marines in action during the battle of Kerch.

Ivan Shagin: A political commissar directing the fighting ▶

Mikhail Savin: Cavalry attack on the Smolensk front, September 1942

Dmitri Baltermants: Infantry attack on the Smolensk front, 1942

58 **Dmitri Baltermants: Kerch**

Mikhail Trakhman: Kerch

Anatoli Garanin: A Beethoven recital, Crimean front, 1942

Dmitri Baltermants: Searching for loved ones at Kerch

Dmitri Baltermants: Searching for loved ones

Dmitri Baltermants: Grief

66 **Mikhail Trakhman: A pause in the fighting**

Alexander Uzlyan: Five photographs of the Black Sea marines in action, 1942 67

STALINGRAD, SEPTEMBER 1942-JANUARY 1943

The defeat at Kharkov left the entire Soviet southern front wide open. The Germans hastened to take advantage of this. The German generals favoured a renewed offensive against Moscow. Hitler rejected this idea. Instead he ordered an advance on Stalingrad far away to the south-east. Its capture would cut communications between central Russia and the oilfields of the Caucasus. Hitler had further ambitious aims. Once Stalingrad was taken the German armies would wheel north and encircle Moscow or they would wheel south and secure the Caucasian oilfields. Perhaps they would attempt both at once.

The German advance began on 28 June. A month later Hitler rang up his Army Chief of Staff, Halder, and said, 'The Russian is finished.' Halder replied, 'I must admit, it looks like it.' The Russians had now learnt how to retreat. There were no fresh encirclements. The Russian armies survived, though weakened. On 23 August the Germans under Paulus reached the Volga. Stalingrad straggled for some twenty miles along the river's banks. Hence it could not be encircled. It had to be taken by assault. Fierce combats went on for three months, with the Russians contesting every yard. German strength was gradually worn down. Soviet reinforcements increased.

The left flank of the Germans was covered by the river Don and guarded only by the armies of their allies, the Rumanians and the Hungarians. The German generals believed that the Russians were incapable of a new offensive. They were wrong. On 19 September Stalin agreed to Zhukov's proposal to take the Germans in the rear. Few reinforcements were sent to Stalingrad. The bulk went far away behind the German lines.

On 19 November six Russian armies broke through the Rumanian and German lines north and south of Stalingrad. On 23 November the two attacking forces met near Kalach. It was now the turn of Paulus to be encircled. Hitler forbade any withdrawal and Paulus obeyed. Attempts were made to relieve the encircled armies. They failed. On 31 January 1943, Paulus, who had just been made a field marshal, surrendered. A quarter of a million German soldiers were lost. 91,000 went into captivity from which only 6,000 returned. It was the turn of the tide.

Georgi Zelma had a long experience of war. He had witnessed the German capture of Odessa and the German victory at Kharkov. From there he went to Stalingrad where he remained during the four months of fighting. His pictures are the main record of that savage time. Later Zelma had the satisfaction of witnessing the liberation of his home city, Odessa.

Georgi Lipskerov was the oldest cameraman of the war. His record is unique in another way. He did not go to the war. It came to him. Presumably too old to go to the front, he remained in Stalingrad as a reserve officer and editor of an army newspaper. Suddenly he found himself in the front line. He took part in the fighting there. At its end he had a stroke of luck. Wearing an ordinary army greatcoat, he was present when Paulus surrendered. Paulus, not recognizing him as a journalist, made no attempt to strike a dignified air. The result was Lipskerov's photograph of a field marshal at the moment of defeat (p. 82), a photograph which at once went round the world.

Georgi Zelma: Stalingrad, February 1943 ▶

74 **Yakov Ryumkin: Fighting in the Red October factory, Stalingrad**

Yakov Ryumkin: Reinforcements entering Stalingrad, September 1942 ▶

76 **Georgi Zelma: House-to-house fighting in Stalingrad, where 600,000 Germans died**

78 **Georgi Zelma: Fighting in the suburbs of Stalingrad, 1942**

80

Georgi Zelma: December 1942
Georgi Lipskerov: House-to-house fighting, December 1942 ▶

Georgi Lipskerov:
Field Marshal Paulus is taken prisoner of war at Beketovka near Stalingrad, February 1943
Yakov Ryumkin:
House-to-house fighting, December 1942 ▶

Georgi Zelma: First bread for the prisoners, February 1943

Georgi Zelma: A mass grave of Soviet defenders, Stalingrad, January 1943

THE YEARS OF VICTORY, 1943-4

After the victory of Stalingrad Soviet armies began an advance that was to carry them into Germany and central Europe. They fought two great battles: at Kursk in July 1943 when the German army was for the first time decisively beaten in the field, and against the German Army Group Centre in June 1944 when the Germans lost 28 divisions and 350,000 German prisoners were taken. After each victory the Russians switched to another front and kept their advance moving steadily forwards.

Each of the two years had its own character. 1943 was the year of liberation when Soviet soil was cleared of the enemy. There were rejoicings and family reunions. 1944 was the year of conquest when the Soviet armies reached German soil. Rumania surrendered. Hungary was entered and by January 1945 Soviet forces were in Austria. The difference between the two years is reflected in the photographs. Those of 1943 are still infused with the humanity and grief of the previous years. Those of 1944 record the events of war and the movements of the armies.

Galina Sankova was one of the five women photographers. She had also been trained as a nurse and car mechanic and had often to turn away from her camera work to tend the wounded. Her most striking achievement perhaps was the photograph of Russian children (p. 107) herded into a concentration camp at Petrozavodski by the Germans. Some years later Sankova traced one of the girls in the picture and photographed her again as a university student.

Sankova has said, 'Difficulties don't exist for me and I don't care about bad food or discomfort. I try to overcome all this the same way that men do.' When asked if her male colleagues helped her, she replied, 'I always had to look after myself as they had enough to do worrying about themselves … Maybe there is something feminine in my pictures because after all I am a woman, but I don't really know what it would be as I've been living like a man too long.' Sankova sees her pictures as a single theme: 'On the Trail of Horror'. She concludes, 'I wanted to show future generations all that horror in my photographs.'

Max Alpert also accompanied the army on its great advance. He has given a very human account of his early experiences: 'The first time I was under fire I was unable to take a single picture. I didn't know where to turn or where to look first. When the battle was over, I noticed a striking sight: helmets, lost rifles and discarded ammunition strewn about the trodden ground. I told myself that when I calmed down I would take a picture of that still life. But then everything went black again and there was another volley of fire between us and the enemy. I jumped into a trench where I saw a number of small, grey mice running around. I'm ashamed to admit it but, in spite of the shots being fired all around me, I jumped out of the trench and sought refuge in a nearby crater. Of course, I never took a picture of that still life. It had disappeared.' Alpert's portrait of his combat commander, Battalion Commander A. G. Yeryomenko (p. 87), became a symbol of the victorious advance of the Soviet Army west into Europe.

Max Alpert: The battalion commander, 1942 ▶

88 **Galina Sankova: Spring in the Ukraine, 1943**

Ivan Shagin: Going home, 1943

90 **Mark Redkin: The enemy has gone, Smolensk, autumn 1944**

Arkadi Shaykhet: Thank you, son ▶

Mark Redkin: Home leave, 1943
◄ **Mikhail Savin: Homecoming, Ulyanovo, July 1943**

93

Mark Redkin: Thank you, son

Mark Redkin: Home leave, 1943

Mikhail Savin: German cemetery near Smolensk

Emmanujel Yevzerikhin: Artillery, 1944

Georgi Zelma: Reconnaissance

Max Alpert: Tank attack, 1944

Max Alpert: Partisans, 1944
Max Alpert: Getting across, 1944 ▶

Mikhail Trakhman: Near miss

Ivan Shagin: Direct hit

Dmitri Baltermants: Moving across the Oder, 1944

Rafail Diament: North Sea fleet

Yevgeni Khaldei: Into Austria, April 1945

Left to right:
Mikhail Savin: Königsberg, April 1945
Arkadi Shaykhet: Königsberg 1945
Alexander Ustinov: Poland 1945

BERLIN

The Germans did not take Moscow. The Russians took Berlin. This was their last and, as they felt, their crowning achievement of the war. The Russian advance began on 16 April 1945 with two million men and 6,300 tanks. On 30 April Hitler killed himself and his wife Eva Braun whom he had married the previous day. The commander of the Berlin garrison surrendered on 2 May. There was no formal capitulation. The Russians simply took over the city and ran it until the arrival of Allied contingents to share the task.

Berlin had lost all military significance except as a centre of communications. Its capture was merely symbolic as the end of the Reich, and the supreme symbol was the Reichstag, an empty shell since the fire there in February 1933. Viktor Tyomin, a special correspondent for *Pravda*, was determined to take the first photograph of the Red Flag flying over the Reichstag. The opportunity came on 1 May. Tyomin flew over the Reichstag in the plane assigned to him and took his photograph. But now he had to get it to his paper. The plane had been hit by anti-aircraft fire and the pilot refused to fly it to Moscow.

Tyomin telephoned Marshal Zhukov who agreed to lend him his private plane, on condition that it went no farther than the Polish town of Janov. This would not be in time to catch the next day's edition of the papers. Greatly daring, Tyomin ordered the pilot to fly on to Moscow. At 2 a.m. he delivered his picture to the newspaper office. Meanwhile Zhukov issued an order that Tyomin was to be shot for stealing the plane. The next day Tyomin returned to Berlin with 20,000 copies of *Pravda* which he distributed to his astonished colleagues. He recalls, 'A group of more than sixty correspondents would have liked to tear me in pieces on the spot, and I'm sure that even today, thirty years later, some of them have not forgiven me for what I did.' The photograph (p. 121) was reproduced all over the world. The *News Chronicle* described it as 'one of the historic monuments of war that will live on even in peacetime'.

Finally Tyomin went to face Zhukov, who had not rescinded the order for his execution. Zhukov said: 'You deserve a hero's medal for your action but for your lack of discipline in stealing the aircraft of a front commander, you deserve punishment. Therefore you will only receive the Order of the Red Star.'

◀ **Ivan Shagin: From Himmler's house to the Reichstag, 1 May 1945**

Yevgeni Khaldei: To the centre of Berlin

Vladimir Grebnev: On the way to the Reichstag

118 **Yevgeni Khaldei: Victors' signatures, Berlin 1945**　　　　　　　　　　**Yakov Ryumkin: The banner of victory, Reichstag, 1 May 1945** ▶

122 **Ivan Shagin: Prisoners at the Brandenburg Gate, 1945**

Ivan Shagin: Berlin, 2 May 1945

◀ Yevgeni Khaldei: Stalingrad avenged, Berlin, 2 May 1945.   Vladimir Grebnev: Stalingrad-to-Berlin dance 125

Mikhail Trakhman: Let the soldiers sleep

Dmitri Baltermants: A Tchaikovsky recital, Berlin 1945   127

Georgi Lipskerov: Let the soldiers sleep

Ivan Shagin: The conquerors of Berlin ▶

AFTERMATH

Yevgeni Khaldei: Vienna, April 1945

◀ Max Alpert: Victory Day on Moscow's Red Square, 9 May 1945

Yevgeni Khaldei: Home to ruin, 1942

Yevgeni Khaldei: Berlin, June 1945

Mark Redkin: The end

Georgi Lipskerov: The end

THE PHOTOGRAPHERS

Opposite page: Mark Redkin: Soviet press photographers in front of the Reichstag, June 1945

Max Alpert (b. 1899)
Max Alpert, one of the pioneers of Soviet photo-reportage, published his first photographs in 1924 and, together with A. Shaykhet, G. Petrusov, S. Fridlyand and other photographers of his generation, was responsible for making journalistic photography the equal of other more traditional genres. During the second world war he was a correspondent for TASS and photographed battles of the Fourth Ukrainian Front in Czechoslovakia. In 1959 he became a reporter for the Soviet Information Bureau and later for the Novosti News Agency.

Dmitri Baltermants (b. 1912)
Dmitri Baltermants spent the entire war at the front as a correspondent for *Izvestiya* and the army newspaper, *Na Razgrom vraga (To Destroy the Enemy).*

He photographed the defeat of the Germans near Moscow, the defence of Sevastopol (most notably, the aftermath of the failed offensive at Kerch), the Battle of Stalingrad, the liberation of southern U.S.S.R. and battles in Poland. Today Baltermants is chief press photographer for *Ogonyok* magazine, where he has worked for thirty years. He has also edited several photographic publications. Many of his photographic essays are well known, but most renowned are his pictures of war.

Rafail Diament (b. 1907)
After Diament's first photograph was published in 1927, he started working regularly for the press and, in 1937, moved to Moscow as a professional photographer. Throughout the war he served as a correspondent, reporting on the North Sea Fleet. He retired in 1969 but still publishes occasionally.

Anatoli Garanin (b. 1912)

A photographer with a rich cultural background, Anatoli Garanin's photographic repertoire is not limited to journalism but also includes such genres as scenic and theatre photography. During the war he was a reporter for *Frontovaya Illyustracia*. He now works as a special correspondent for *Sovetsky Soyuz* and is also affiliated with the Moscow theatre, Na Tagantse, where a permanent exhibition of his theatrical photographs is housed.

Vladimir Grebnev (b. 1907)

Grebnev began photographing in the 1930s as a reporter. When war broke out, he joined the staff of the army newspaper, *Krasnaya zvezda (Red Star)*, and was later transferred, at his own request, to the front-line newspaper, *Frontovik (The Front-line Fighter)*. He was one of the photographers of the Soviet Banner of Victory that was hoisted over the Reichstag. After the war, Grebnev remained for several years in the Soviet zone of Germany as a press photographer. He later became a sports reporter in the U.S.S.R.

Yevgeni Khaldei (b. 1916)

As a reporter for *Pravda* and the TASS News Agency during the second world war, Khaldei took part in the largest battles on Soviet soil. The last year of the war took him to Rumania, Bulgaria, Yugoslavia, Hungary, Austria and finally — like so many of his colleagues — to Berlin. He was one of the photographers at the Potsdam Conference and the Nuremberg trials. His pictures of the war have been exhibited many times both at home and abroad. Khaldei now works for *Sovyetskaya Kultura (Soviet Culture)* magazine.

Boris Kudoyarov (1903–73)

One of the founders of Soviet press photography, Kudoyarov joined the ranks of the Red Army during the Civil War at the age of seventeen as platoon deputy commander. Before the second world war, Kudoyarov worked for several magazines and news agencies; during the war he was a special correspondent for Moscow's *Komsomolskaya Pravda*. He was the only reporter to spend almost the entire 900 days of the siege in Leningrad, and his photographic epic of the city is a remarkable record of the battles as well as everyday life in the city. In 1973, Kudoyarov was killed in a car accident while photographing in Tashkent, Uzbekistan.

Georgi Lipskerov (1896–1977)
Lipskerov was one of the oldest cameramen of the second world war. He joined the staff of an army newspaper when he was almost fifty and spent the entire war at the front. His prior experience as an active sportsman was good preparation for life in the front lines. Until his death he continued to work as a photographer for various publications.

Mark Redkin (b. 1908)
Redkin's work for the army newspaper, *Krasnaya zvezda*, trained him as a war correspondent. During the war Redkin worked for TASS and *Frontovaya Illyustracia*. He photographed, among many other important events, the surrender of Germany. The war did not end in Berlin for Redkin. He visited liberated Prague and was later sent to the Japanese front. He now works for Planeta, a Moscow publishing house.

Yakov Ryumkin (b. 1913)
Ryumkin began to publish photographs in 1926. He worked for *Pravda* and *Ogonyok*, and is now with *Selskaya Nov (Agricultural News)* magazine. During the war he was a *Pravda* correspondent.

Galina Sankova (b. 1904)
Galina Sankova is the best known of the five women who were photographic reporters during the war. Involved in photography since the 1930s, she has succeeded in equalling the achievements of her male colleagues in spite of the many difficulties she encountered as a woman attempting to reach the front. She photographed the Western, Briansk and Don fronts near Stalingrad and the northern offensive of 1944 in besieged Leningrad for *Frontovaya Illyustracia*. Often laying aside her camera to serve as a nurse, Galina Sankova was twice seriously wounded herself. She is now on the staff of *Ogonyok* magazine.

Mikhail Savin (b. 1915)

Mikhail Savin began his professional career in 1939 as a correspondent in Byelorussia for the TASS News Agency. During the war he was a reporter for the newspaper of the western part of the front, *Krasnoarmeyskaya Pravda (Red Army Pravda)*. Since 1945 he has worked for *Ogonyok* magazine.

Ivan Shagin (b. 1904)

Shagin's acquaintance with Roman Karmen, who was to become an outstanding photographer at the front, influenced him to become a photographer. Between 1932 and 1950, Shagin was the chief reporter for *Komsomolskaya Pravda*. Since 1950 he has worked for various Soviet publishing houses.

Arkadi Shaykhet (1898–1959)

Arkadi Shaykhet was one of the leaders of the group of Soviet press photographers who came to the fore after the Revolution of 1917. He was one of the initiators of the movement in the 1920s and 1930s that elevated photographic reportage to the same level as literary reportage. His picture, 'Thank you, son', ranks with Capa's 'Fallen fighter' and Baltermants's 'Grief' as one of the most effective protests against the horrors of war ever photographed.

Mikhail Trakhman (1918–1976)

When war broke out Trakhman was a special correspondent for TASS. Later he joined the Soviet

Information Bureau. He photographed not only at various fronts but also behind the enemy lines. For many years he was a special correspondent for the *Literaturnaya Gazeta*, but his main interest was the editing of pictorial books about the second world war.

Viktor Tyomin (b. 1908)

Viktor Tyomin has been a reporter for various publications and has photographed in all parts of the U.S.S.R. and in twenty-eight foreign countries. He was the first to photograph the Soviet Banner of Victory over the Reichstag and was one of eight reporters in the world present at the execution of the major Nazi war criminals after the Nuremberg trial. In addition to being present at all fronts during the second world war, he also took part in the fighting in Finland and was present at the surrenders of Germany and Japan. He is now correspondent for special assignments for the U.S.S.R. Press Centre.

Emmanujel Yevzerikhin (b. 1911)

During the second world war, Yevzerikhin was a photographer for TASS, but the aesthetic quality of his photographs was not appreciated until after peace had been declared. He is now a lecturer at the Peoples' University of Photography in Moscow and is also a free-lance reporter for TASS.

Alexander Ustinov (b. 1909)

Ustinov has spent half his life, including the war years, as a correspondent for *Pravda*. During the last two years of the war he was at the First Ukrainian Front, where he photographed the fighting by the First Czechoslovak Army Corps in the autumn of 1944 and the liberation of Czechoslovakia by the Red Army. He also visited Leningrad during the siege and photographed the meeting of Soviet and American forces on the Elbe near Berlin.

Alexander Uzlyan (b. 1908)

Alexander Uzlyan was a staff photographer for *Izvestiya, Pravda* and *Ogonyok* magazine. During the second world war, he was assigned to the Black Sea Fleet (known as 'Black Death' to the Germans) as a correspondent for the Soviet Information Bureau. He devoted a series of photographs to them as well as a book of memoirs. His photographs, which capture the bravery of the marines, give an impression of movement that is almost film-like.

Georgi Zelma (b. 1906)

In the 1920s and 1930s, Georgi Zelma was active in the development of modern Soviet photo-reportage. He began photographing the war as a reporter for *Izvestiya* near Odessa, and later took part in the fighting on all fronts. His pictures of the Battle of Stalingrad merit special mention. When the war ended, Zelma was sent on many photographic assignments abroad and has published several pictorial books, including one on the defence of Stalingrad.